JACK WHITE
BLUNDERBUSS

2 Missing Pieces

7 Sixteen Saltines

12 Freedom at 21

17 Love Interruption

21 Blunderbuss

25 Hypocritical Kiss

28 Weep Themselves to Sleep

37 I'm Shakin'

44 Trash Tongue Talker

49 Hip (Eponymous) Poor Boy

53 I Guess I Should Go to Sleep

57 On and On and On

65 Take Me with You When You Go

This book was approved by Jack White
Cover photo by Jo McCaughey and Andrea Westmoreland
Transcribed by Jeff Jacobson

Cherry Lane Music Company
Director of Publications/Project Editor: Mark Phillips

ISBN 978-1-60378-972-1

Visit our website at www.cherrylaneprint.com

MISSING PIECES

Words and Music by
Jack White

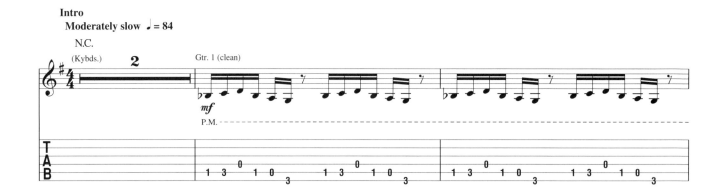

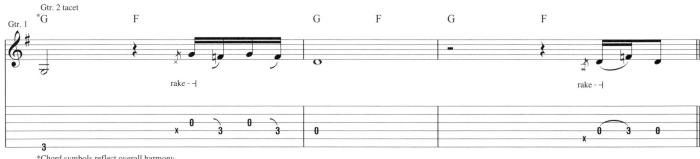

*Chord symbols reflect overall harmony.

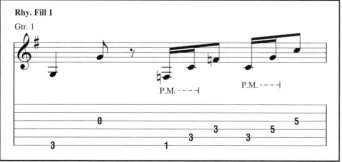

Chorus

Gtr. 1: w/ Rhy. Fig. 1 (1st 2 meas.)

Oak floor, soft pine bed-room door, yeah. Speak eas-y; make her mine if she's bored, yeah. __

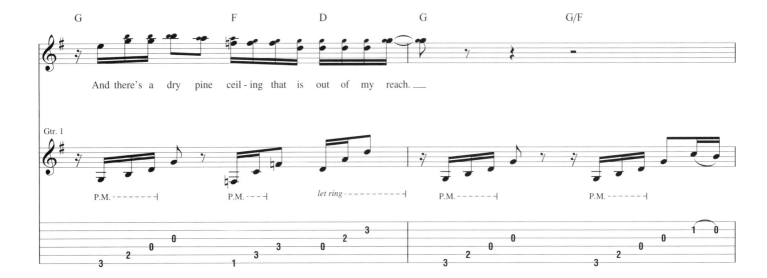

And there's a dry pine ceil-ing that is out of my reach. __

Gtr. 1

P.M. ------- | P.M. --- | let ring --------- | P.M. ------- | P.M. ------ |

D.S. al Coda

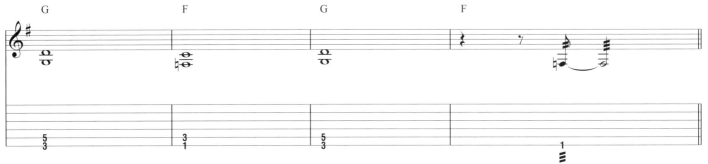

Coda

Guitar Solo

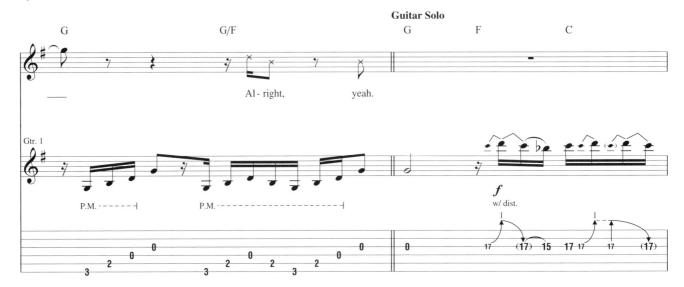

Al-right, yeah.

Gtr. 1

P.M. ------- | P.M. ------------------ |

f

w/ dist.

4

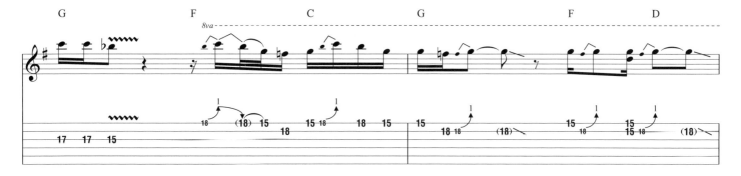

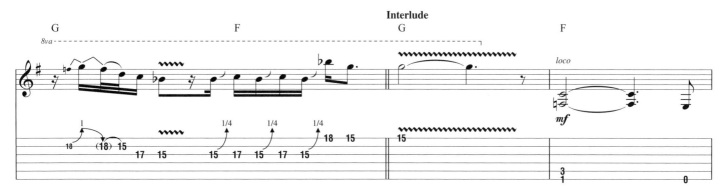

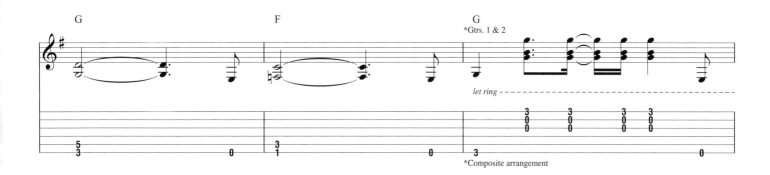

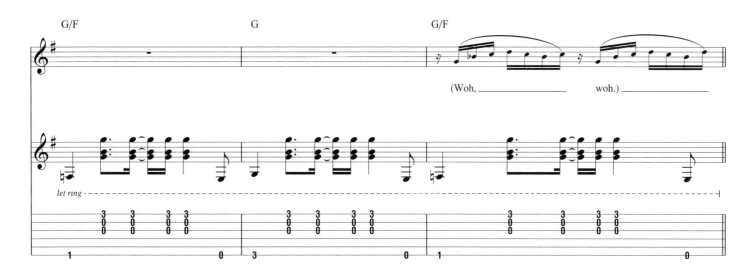

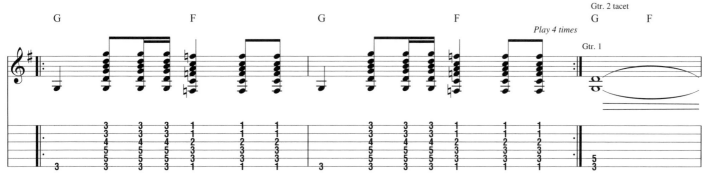

SIXTEEN SALTINES

Words and Music by
Jack White

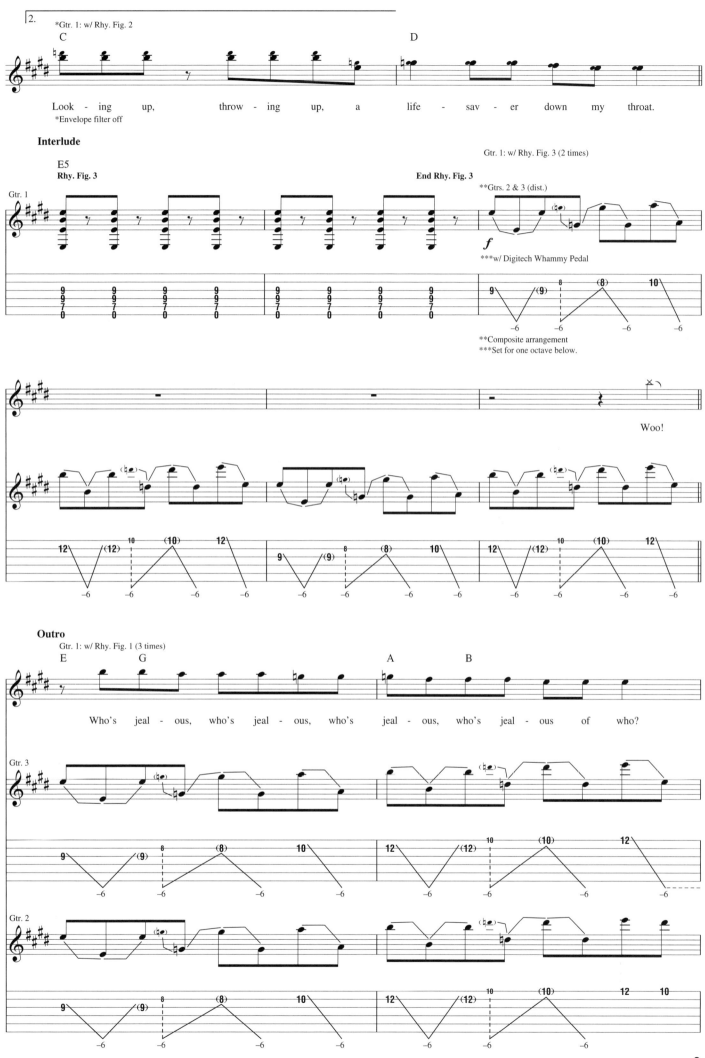

Who's jeal - ous, who's jeal - ous, who's jeal - ous, who's jeal - ous of who?

Whammy Pedal off

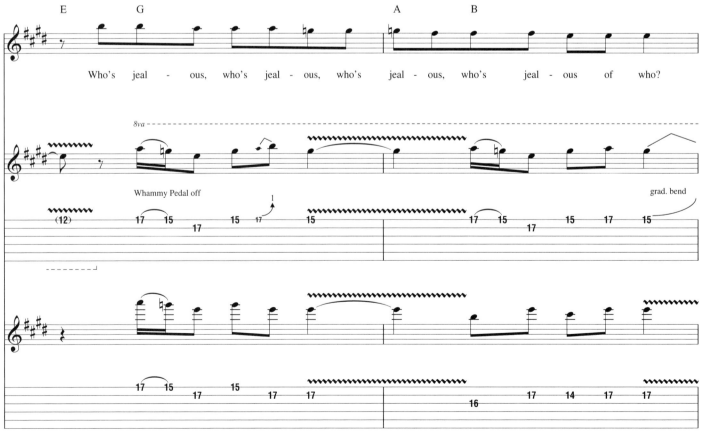

Who's jeal - ous, who's jeal - ous, who's jeal - ous, who's jeal - ous of who?

Whammy Pedal off

grad. bend

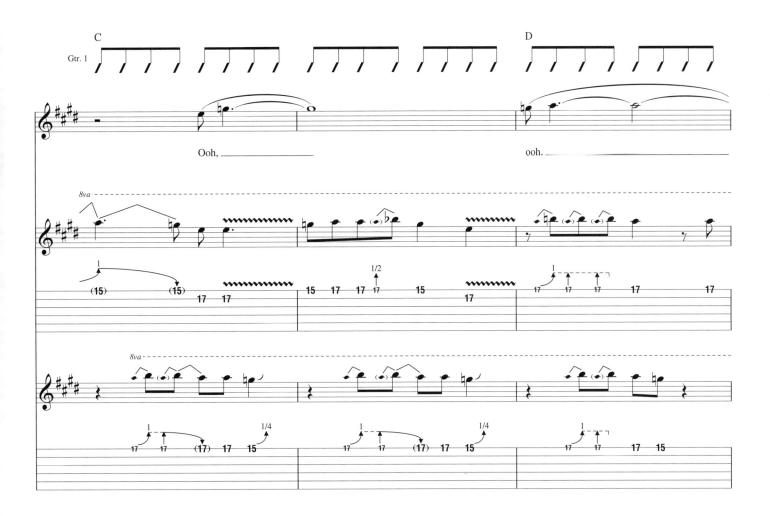

Ooh, _____ ooh. _____

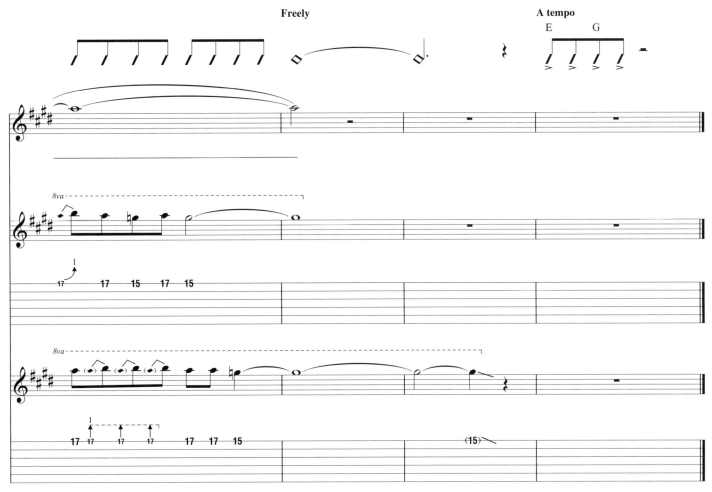

FREEDOM AT 21

Words and Music by
Jack White

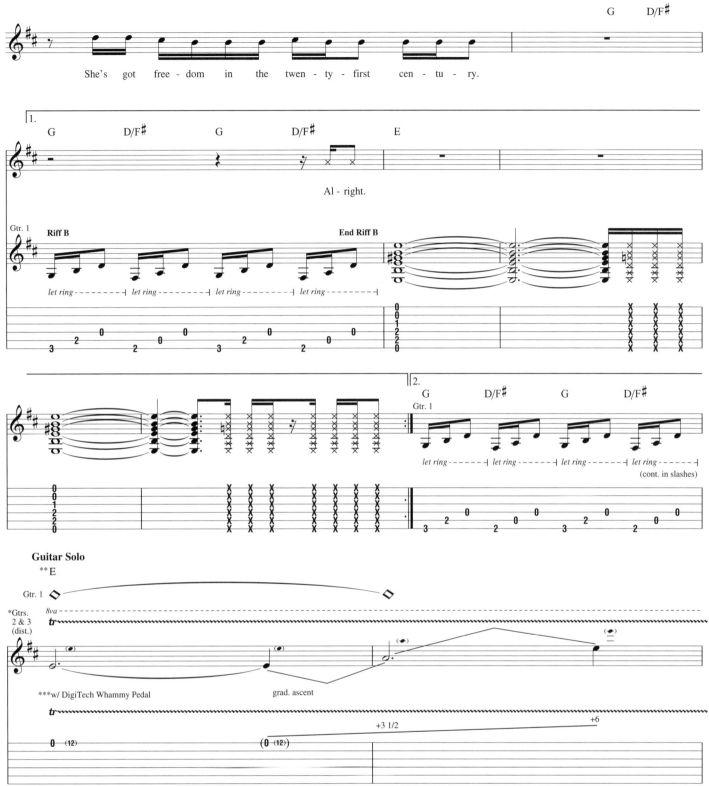

She's got free-dom in the twen-ty-first cen-tu-ry.

Al - right.

Guitar Solo

*Composite arrangement

  **See top of first page of song for chord diagram pertaining to rhythm slashes.

  ***Set for one octave above.

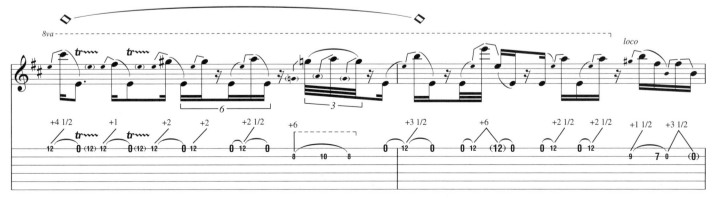

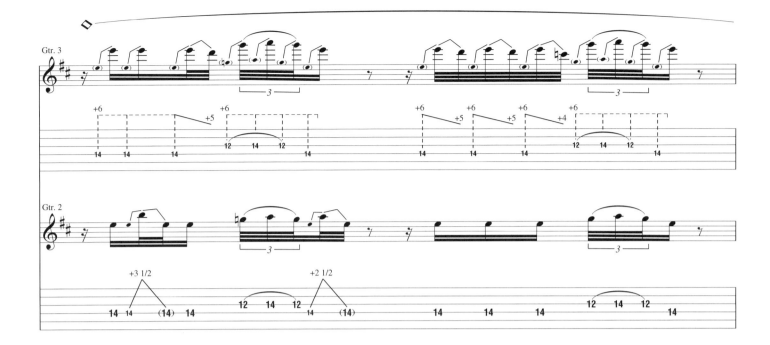

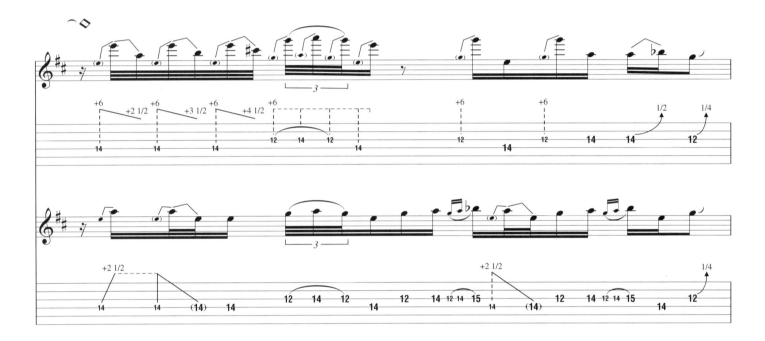

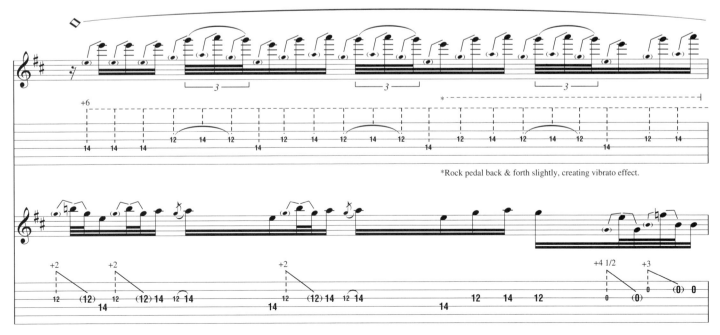

*Rock pedal back & forth slightly, creating vibrato effect.

14

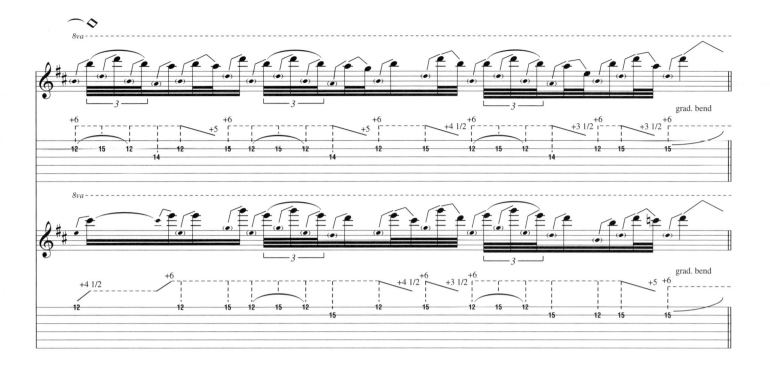

Interlude

Gtr. 1: w/ Riff A

Gtr. 3 tacet

N.C.

Hey!   Hey!   Hey!

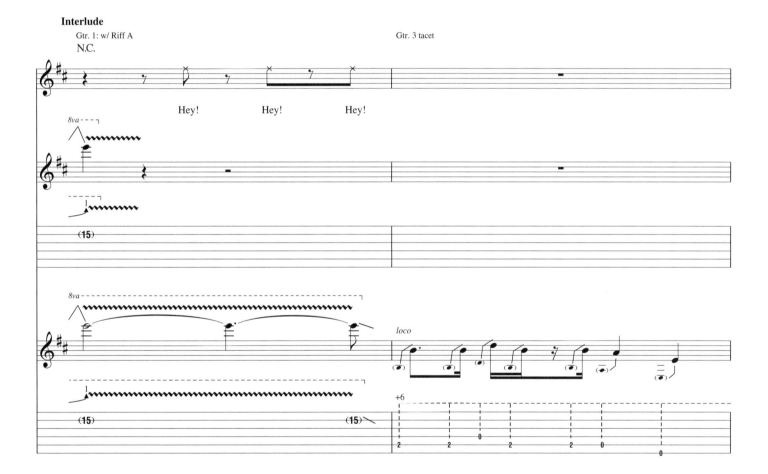

loco

Gtr. 2

G   Dadd4/F#

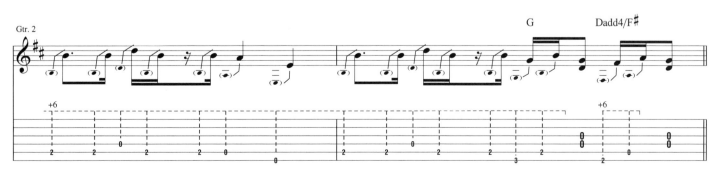

LOVE INTERRUPTION

Words and Music by
Jack White

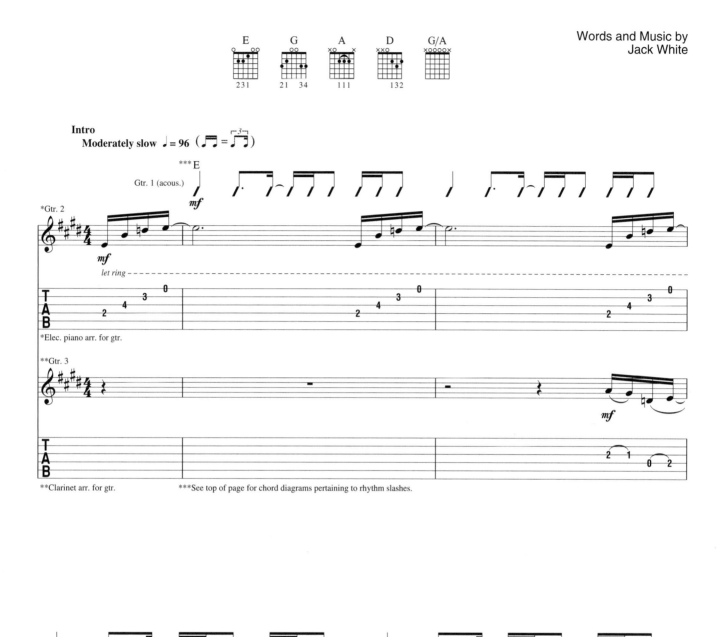

Intro
Moderately slow ♩ = 96

*Elec. piano arr. for gtr.

**Clarinet arr. for gtr.   ***See top of page for chord diagrams pertaining to rhythm slashes.

BLUNDERBUSS

Words and Music by
Jack White

flew. We left your man___ a - lone in drag,___ laugh - ing there___ at

us. A ro - man - tic bust,___ a blun - der turned___ ex - plo - sive blun - der - buss.

Gtr. 2: w/ Riff A (4 times)

*D Cadd9 G D Gtr. 2: w/ Riff A (2 times) D

Rhy. Fig. 1 End Rhy. Fig. 1 Rhy. Fill 1 End Rhy. Fill 1

Gtr. 1

w/ pick Play 4 times

*See top of first page of song for chord diagrams pertaining to rhythm slashes.

Verse

Gtr. 1 tacet Gtr. 2: w/ Riff A (2 times)
N.C. N.C.

2. An an - cient grand___ ho - tel of Per - sian

thread and i - vo - ry. And when your man___ would turn his head, _ I'd see you look___ at

Gtr. 1: w/ Rhy. Fig. 1 (2 times)
D D Cadd9 G D

Gtr. 1

me. ____ Pools of brown___ and sea of red___ and de - mons in___ your pock - et. ____ That

Cadd9 G D

same ro - mance___ per - formed a dance___ in - side a sil - ver lock - et.

Gtr. 2 Riff B End Riff B

HYPOCRITICAL KISS

Words and Music by
Jack White

strong e-nough to for-get a-bout all ___ that I've been ___ through.

And it sounds ob-scene, _ but loud words nev-er both-er me like ___ they do ___

___ to you.

Gtr. 1
Rhy. Fig. 3

let ring ---------- | let ring ---------- | let ring ----------

End Rhy. Fig. 3

Verse
Gtr. 1: w/ Rhy. Fig. 1 (3 times)

2. You're the boy that talks ___ but says noth-ing, a big game to the ones that you think-'ll be-lieve ___

___ you. But you don't know how to read ___ the

look on my face when it says, "Yeah, I've read that book, ___ too." ___

And who the hell's im - pressed ___ by you? I want names of the peo - ple that we know that are fall -

ing for this. You would sell your own moth - er out, ___ and

then be - tray ___ your dead broth - er with an - oth - er hyp - o - crit - i - cal kiss. ___

Oh,

Outro

yeah.
(Sing 1st time only)

WEEP THEMSELVES TO SLEEP

Words and Music by
Jack White

Am   E   D

Intro
Moderately slow ♩ = 88

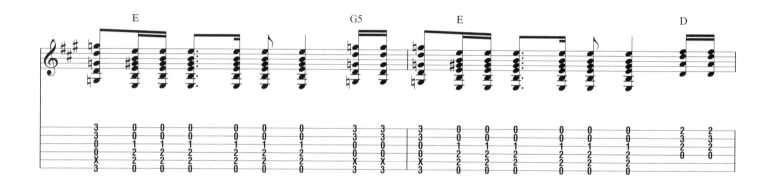

*Gtr. 1 (elec.) w/ dist.; Gtr. 2 (acous.). Composite arrangement

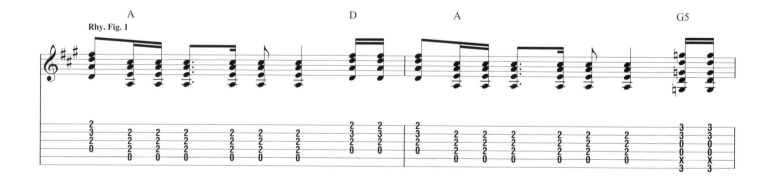

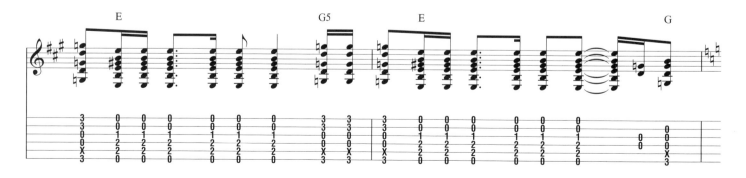

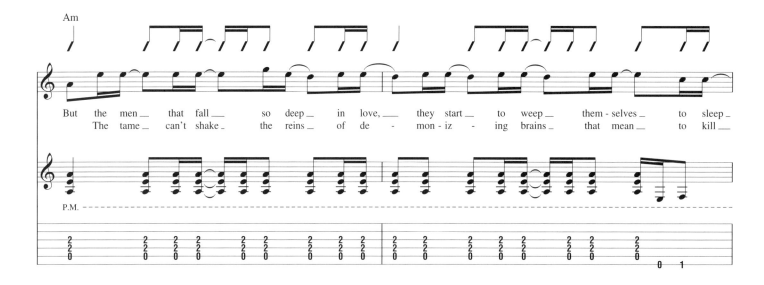

But the men＿ that fall ＿ so deep ＿ in love, ＿ they start ＿ to weep ＿ them-selves ＿ to sleep ＿
The tame ＿ can't shake ＿ the reins ＿ of de - mon - iz - ing brains ＿ that mean ＿ to kill ＿

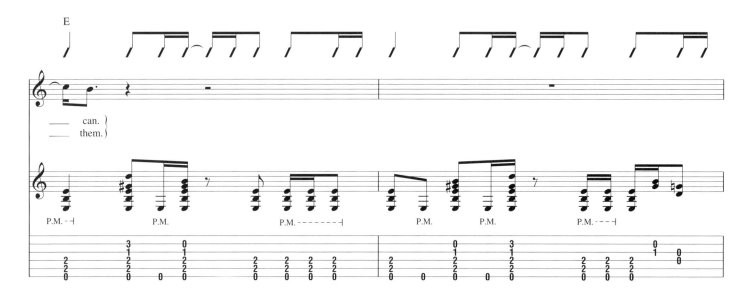

＿ can. 〉
＿ them. 〉

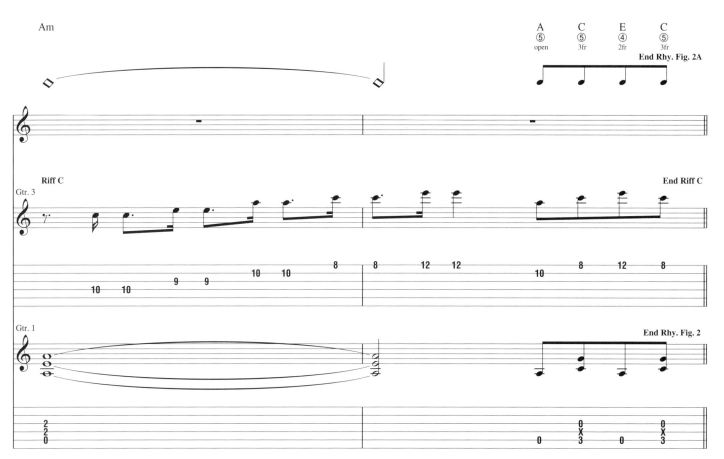

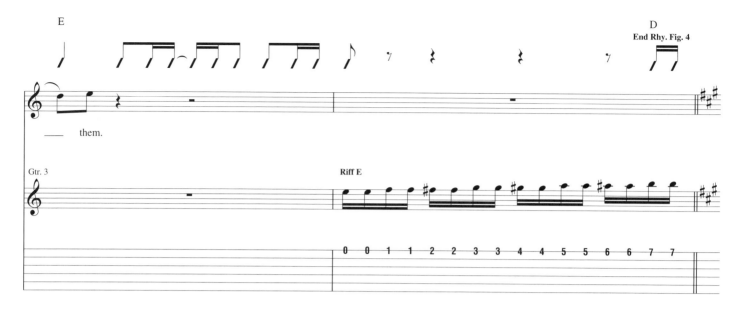

them.

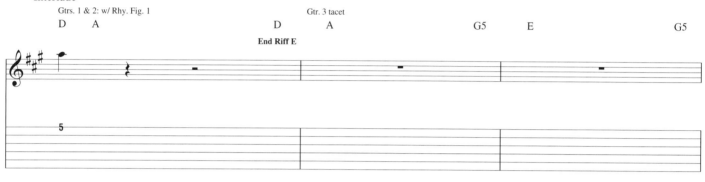

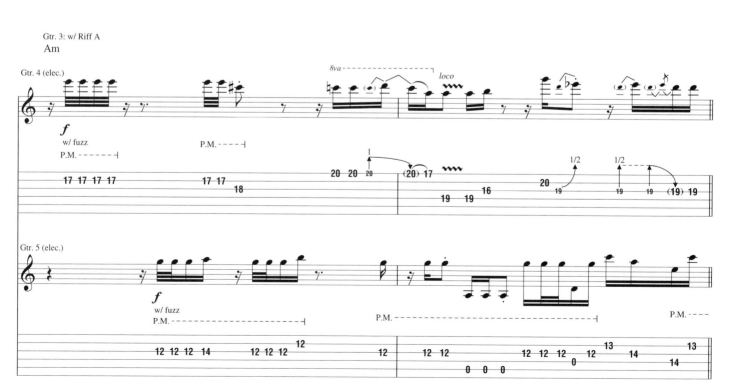

Guitar Solo

Gtrs. 1 & 2: w/ Rhy. Figs. 2 & 2A
Gtr. 3: w/ Riff B

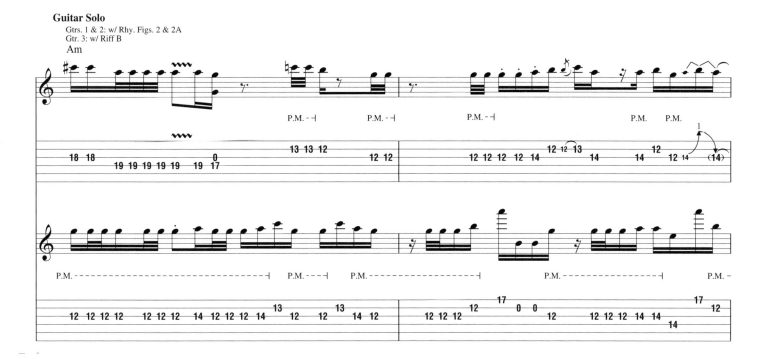

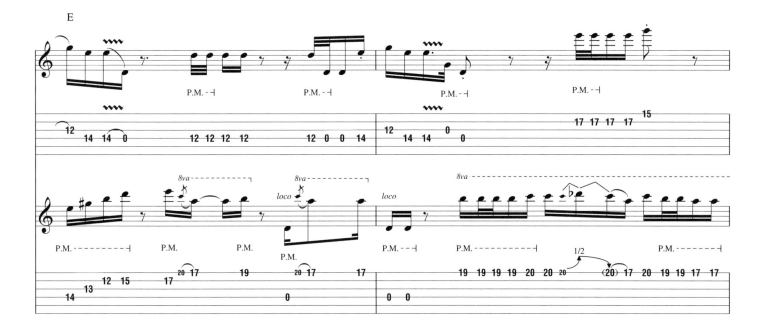

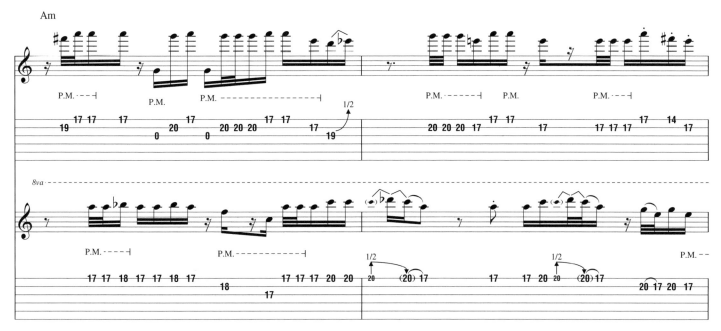

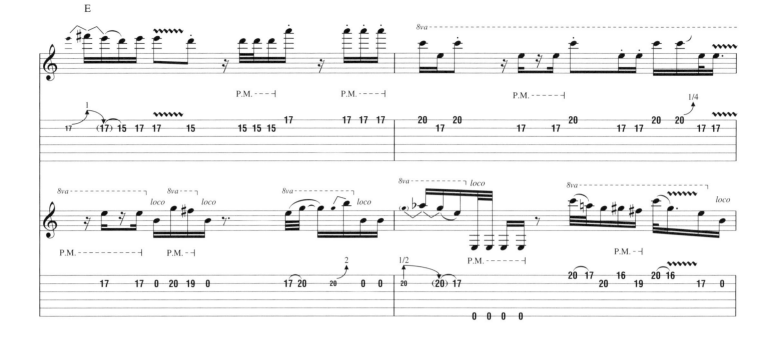

Gtr. 3: w/ Riff C

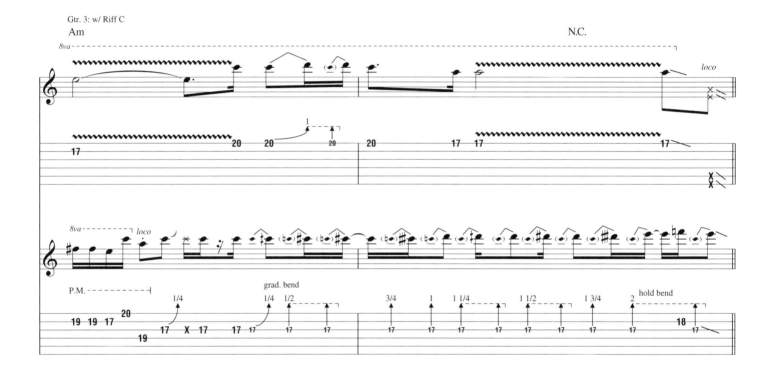

Chorus
Gtrs. 1 & 2: w/ Rhy. Figs. 3 & 3A
Gtr. 3: w/ Riff D
Gtr. 5 tacet

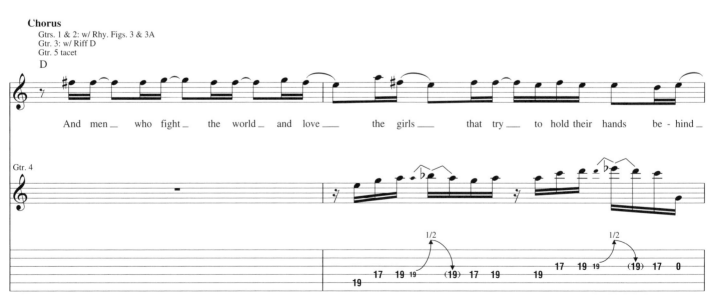

And men ___ who fight ___ the world ___ and love ___ the girls ___ that try ___ to hold their hands ___ be - hind ___

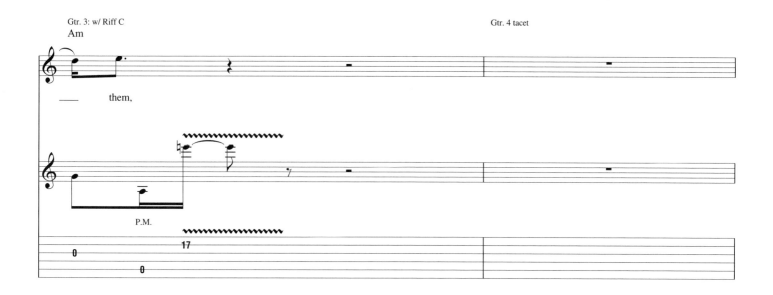

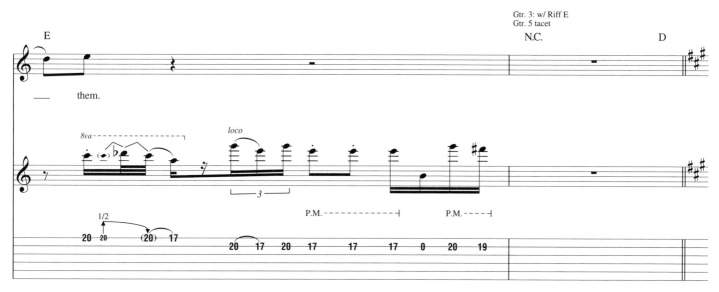

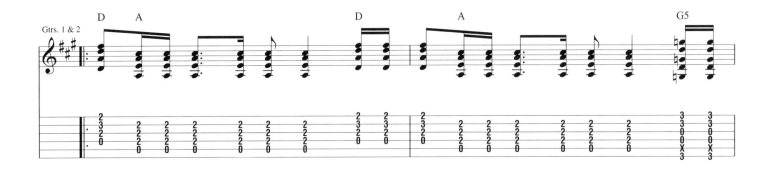

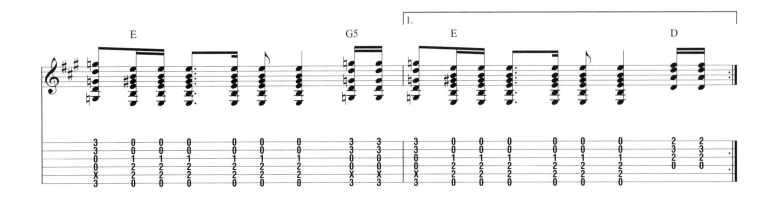

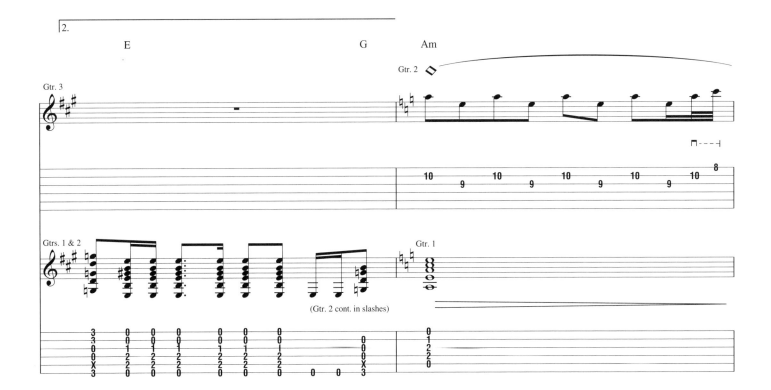

I'M SHAKIN'

Words and Music by
Rudolph Toombs

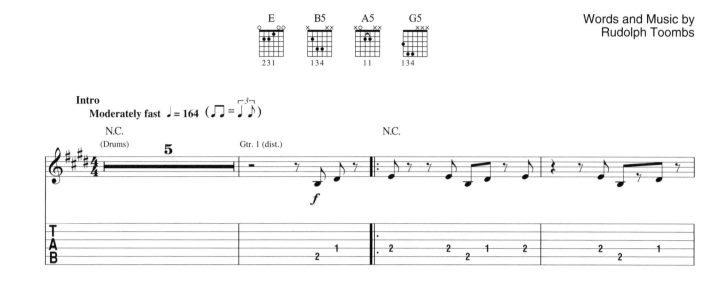

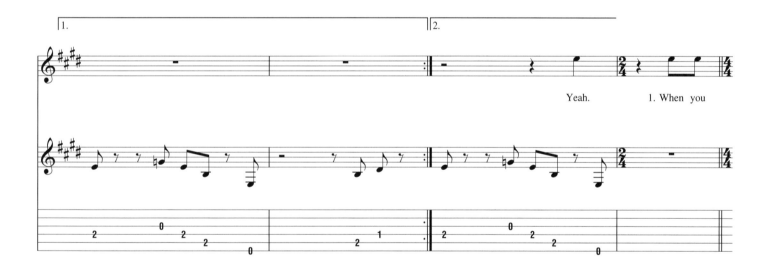

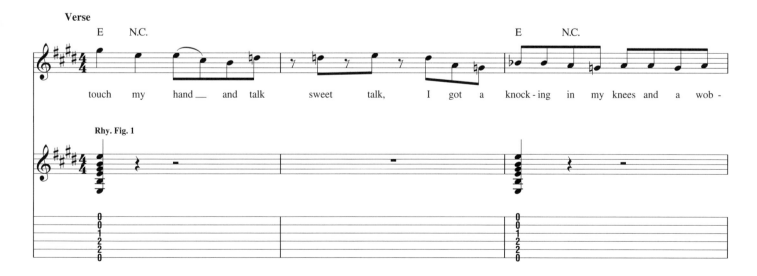

ble in my walk. ___ And I'm trem - blin'. ___

(Ooh.)

End Rhy. Fig. 1   Riff A

That's   right, ___   you   got   me ___   shak - in'. ___

2. When you

End Riff A

Verse

Gtr. 1: w/ Rhy. Fig. 1

E   N.C.   E   N.C.

take   me   in   your   arms ___   and   talk   ro - mance, ___   my   heart   starts - a   do - ing   the   St. ___

Gtr. 1: w/ Riff A

___   Vit - us'   dance. ___   And   I'm   pant - in'. ___

Yeah.

(Ooh.)

Oh, _____   and   I'm   shak - in'. ___

Verse

*E   B5

Rhy. Fig. 2

Gtr. 1

3. Ear - ly   in   the   morn - ing   time, ___

late   in   the   mid - dle   of   the

(Ooh. ___

*See top of first page of song for chord diagrams pertaining to rhythm slashes.

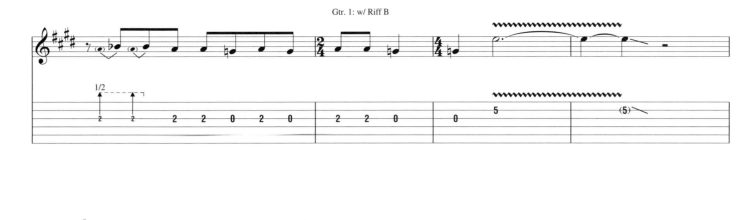

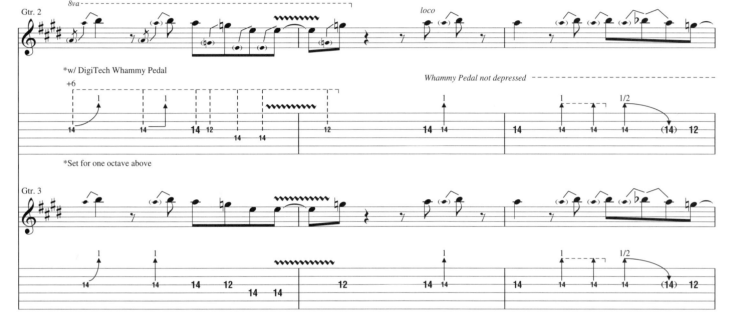

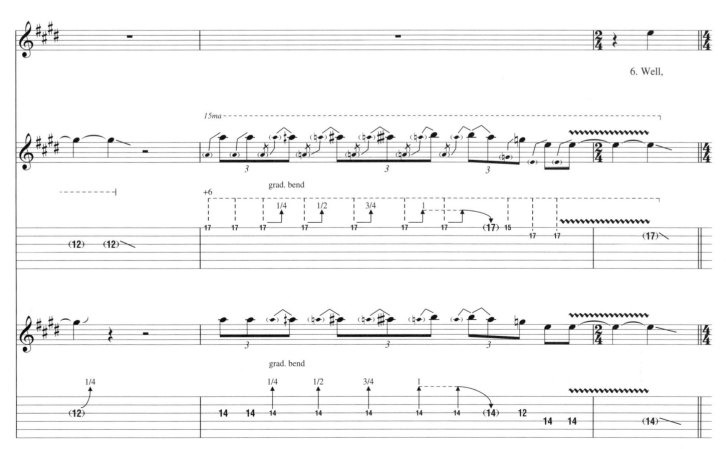

6. Well,

TRASH TONGUE TALKER

Words and Music by
Jack White

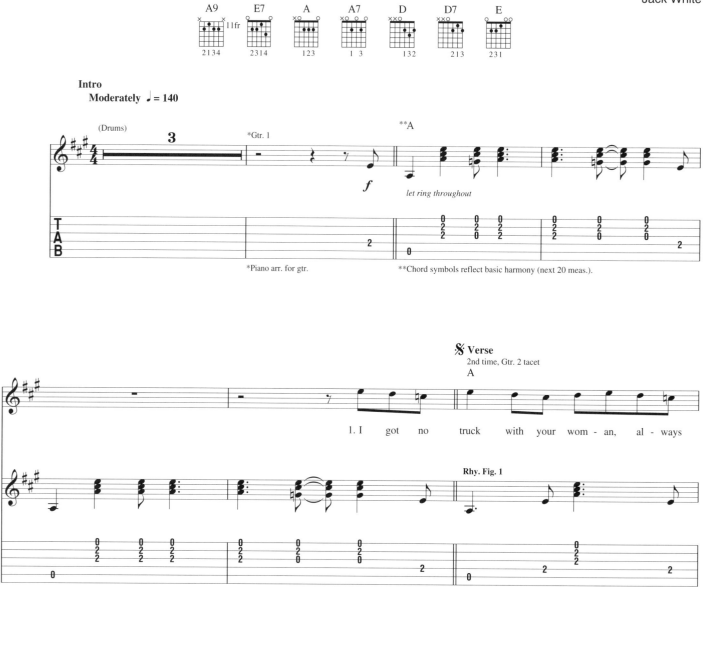

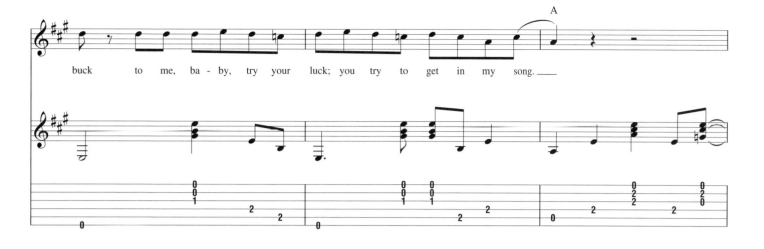

buck to me, ba - by, try your luck; you try to get in my song. ___

2nd time, Gtr. 2: w/ Rhy. Fig. 3

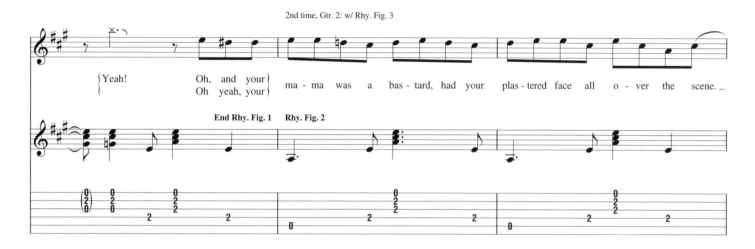

{ Yeah! Oh, and your }
{ Oh yeah, your } ma - ma was a bas - tard, had your plas - tered face all o - ver the scene. _

End Rhy. Fig. 1   **Rhy. Fig. 2**

E7

___ { Oh, And you got }
{ you you got } has - sled by your dad - dy, al - ways

A

push - ing, try'n' to make you come clean. ___ { Yeah.
{ *Vocal tacet* Oh! } 2., 4. You broke your

End Rhy. Fig. 2

HIP (EPONYMOUS) POOR BOY

Words and Music by
Jack White

Verse

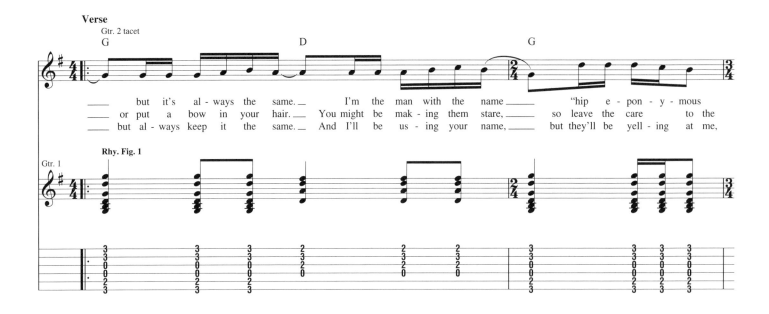

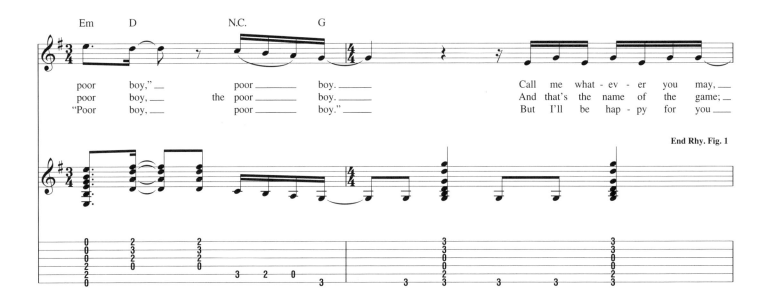

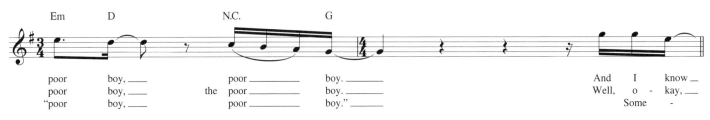

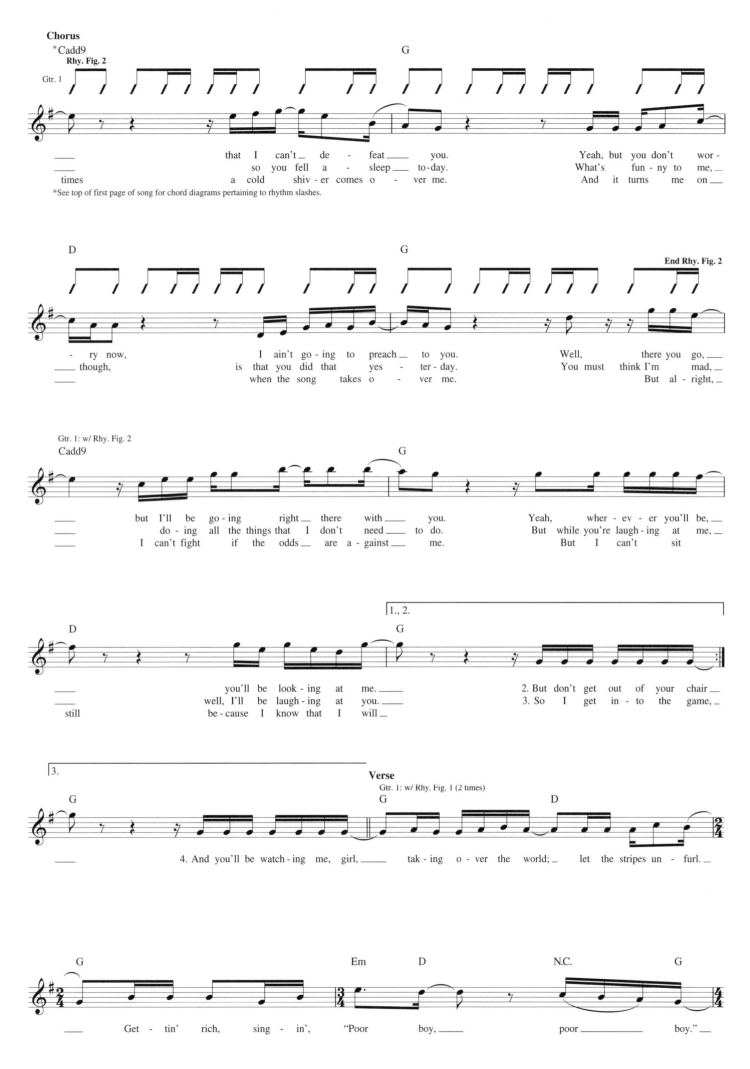

And I'll be com - ing to play; ___ I do it ev - er - y day. ___ And the ti - tle will stay___

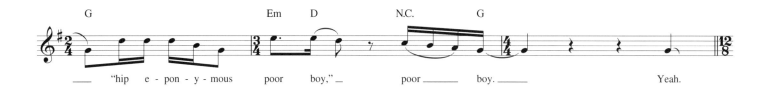

___ "hip e - pon - y - mous poor boy," ___ poor ___ boy. ___ Yeah.

Outro
Tempo I

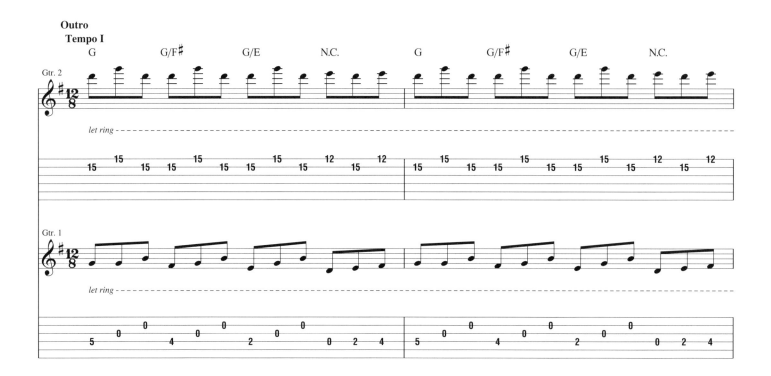

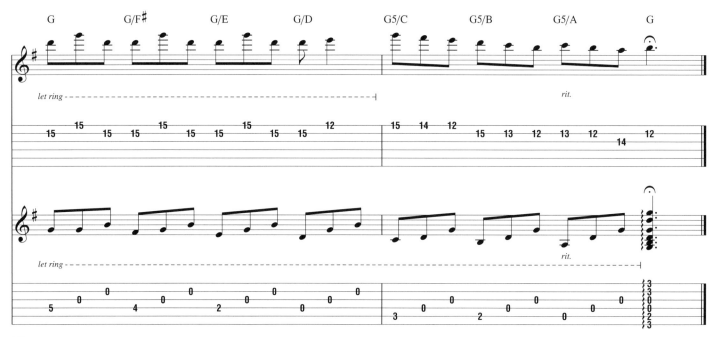

I GUESS I SHOULD GO TO SLEEP

Words and Music by
Jack White

I ain't man-aged to say the right thing __ yet.

(Well, I

guess I should go back to bed.) _____

Yeah.

Piano Solo

Gtr. 1: w/ Rhy. Fig. 1

Gtr. 1

Gtr. 1   Rhy. Fig. 2   End Rhy. Fig. 2

let ring -   *let ring* -

(cont. in slashes)

3. I

guess I should go to sleep; too hard stand-ing on my own two feet. Been

run-ning too long on an end-less street. Well, I

guess I should go to sleep,

sleep, sleep,

sleep.

ON AND ON AND ON

Words and Music by
Jack White

†G played by bass only in all A5/G chords (throughout).

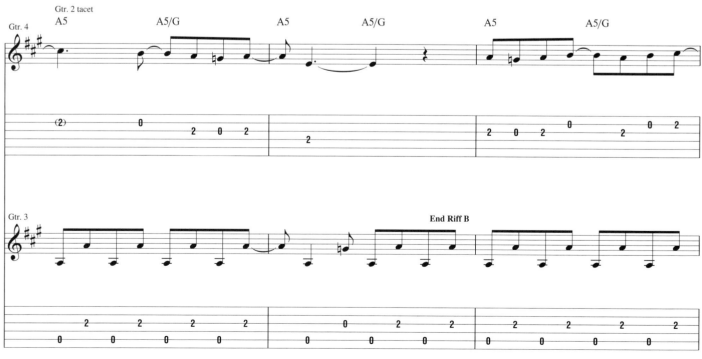

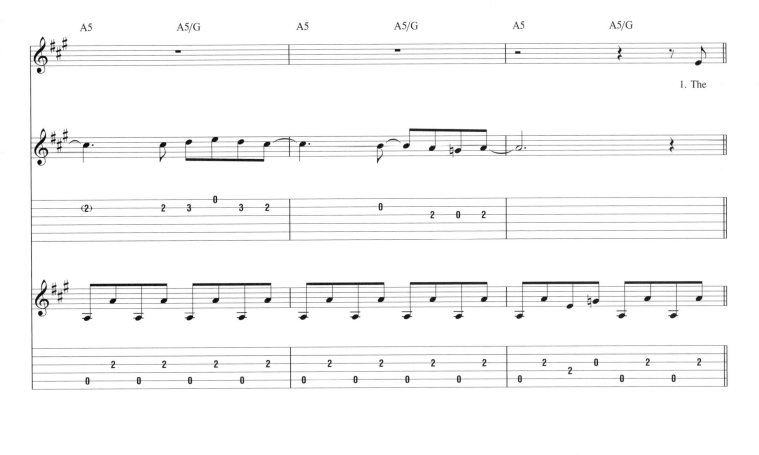

1. The

Verse

Gtr. 3: w/ Riff B

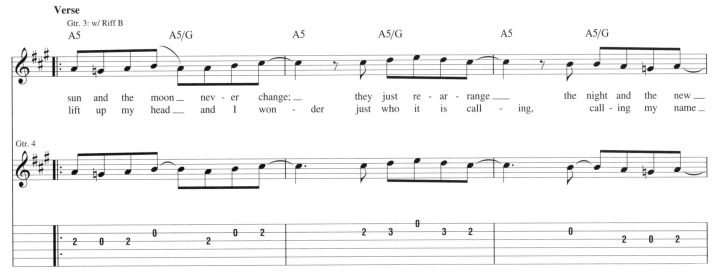

sun and the moon__ nev-er change;__ they just re-ar-range__ the night and the new__
lift up my head__ and I won-der just who it is call-ing, call-ing my name__

Gtr. 4

Gtr. 3: w/ Riff A

__ day. Gold ex-chang-es for sil-ver, and the light on a riv-
__ now. I trip on my way and I blun-der, my head fall-ing un-

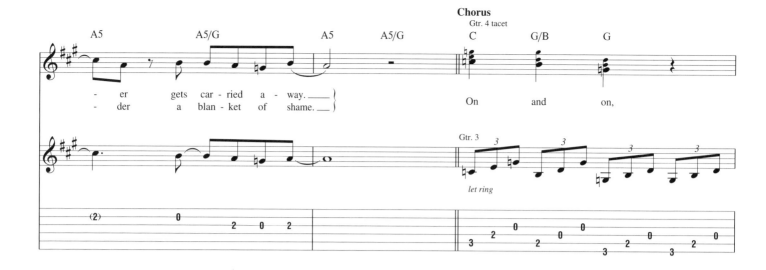

Interlude

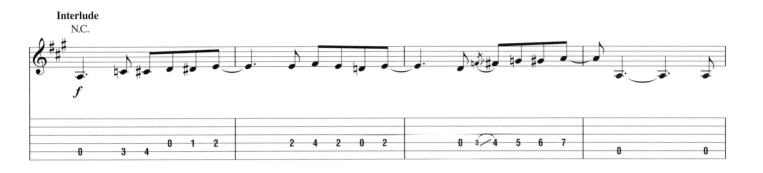

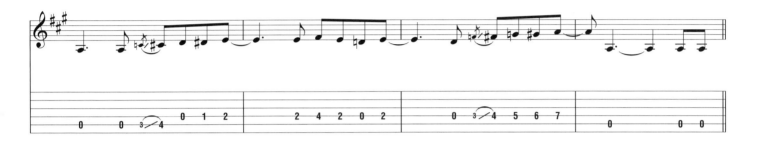

Bridge

High ___ and low may I go, ____ but God on - ly knows ___ just where I am go -

- ing. High and low may I go, ____ but God on - ly knows __

just where I am go - ing.

3. The

Verse

peo - ple a - round__ me won't let____ me be - come what I need ___ to; they want me the same.__

I look at my - self ___ and I want ___ to just cov - er my eyes __

__ and give my - self a new name. __ The stones in the sky ___ nev - er wor-

-ry. They don't have to hur -ry; they move in their own _____ way. But

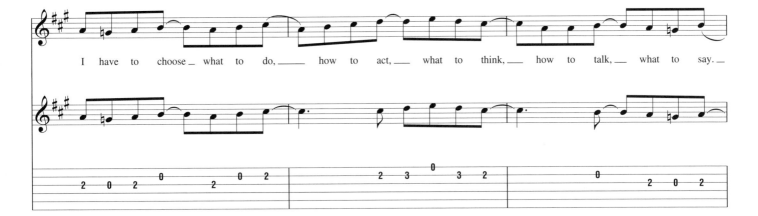

I have to choose _ what to do, _____ how to act, _____ what to think, _____ how to talk, _____ what to say. _____

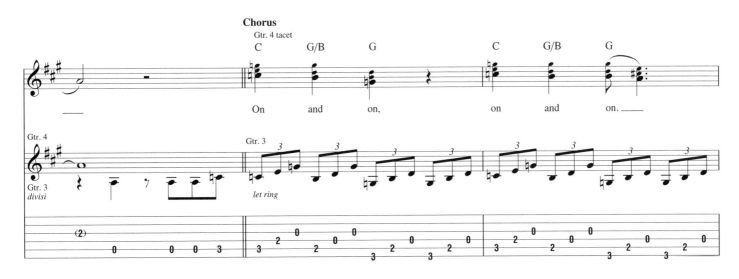

Chorus

Gtr. 4 tacet

C   G/B   G   C   G/B   G

On   and   on,   on   and   on. _____

Gtr. 4

Gtr. 3
divisi

Gtr. 3

let ring

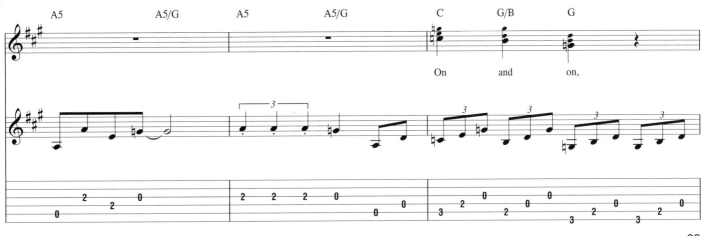

A5   A5/G   A5   A5/G   C   G/B   G

On   and   on,

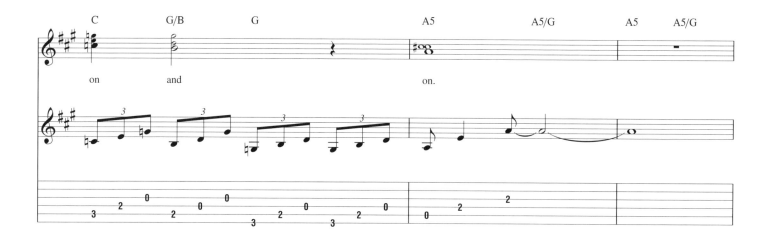

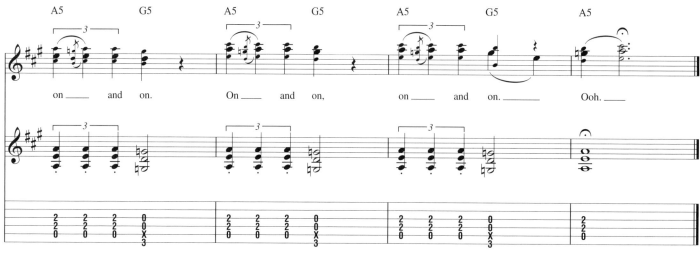

TAKE ME WITH YOU WHEN YOU GO

Words and Music by
Jack White

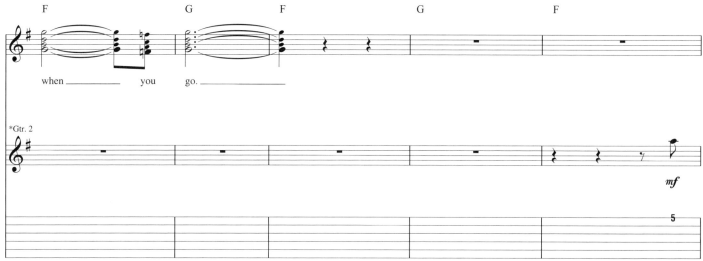

when _____ you go. _____

*Gtr. 2

mf

*Violin arr. for gtr.

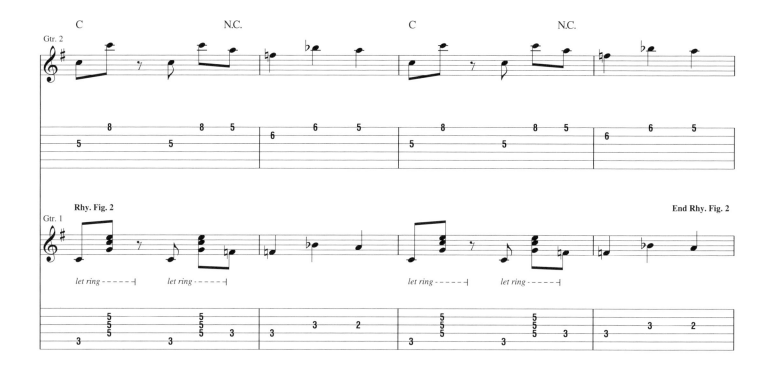

Rhy. Fig. 2

End Rhy. Fig. 2

Gtr. 1

let ring - - - - - ┘   *let ring* - - - - - ┘   *let ring* - - - - - ┘   *let ring* - - - - - ┘

Gtr. 1: w/ Rhy. Fig. 1

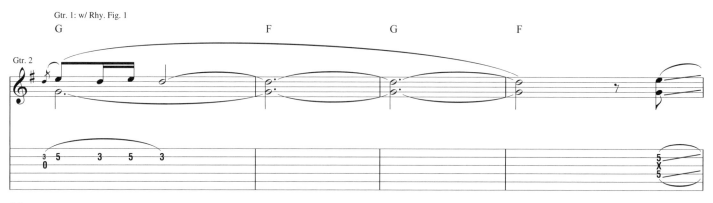

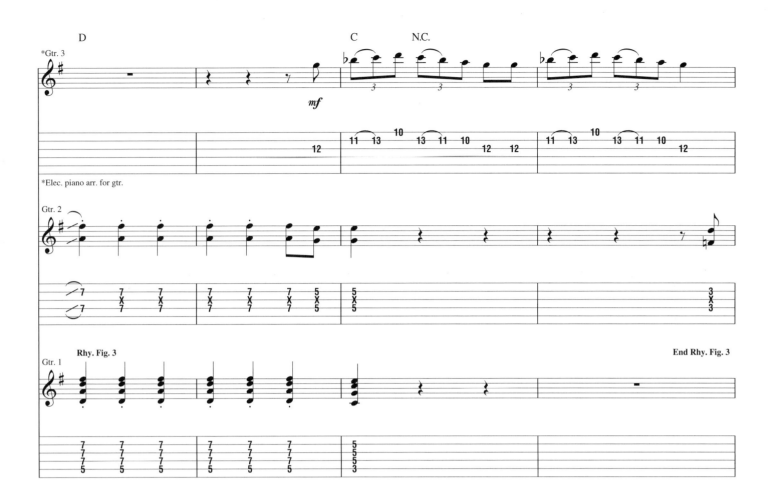

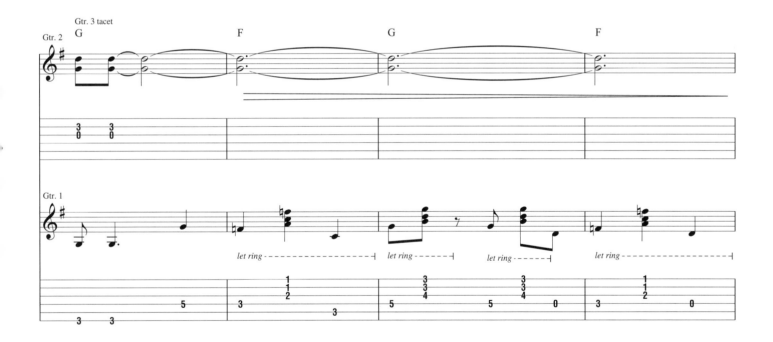

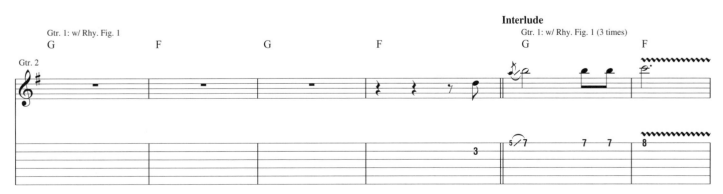

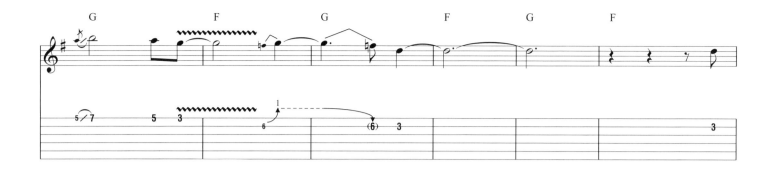

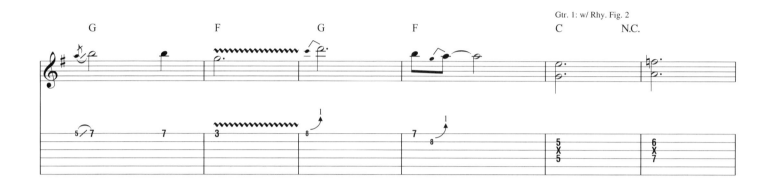

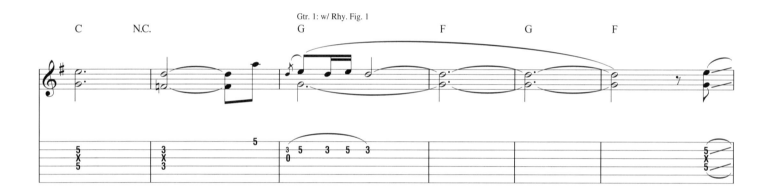

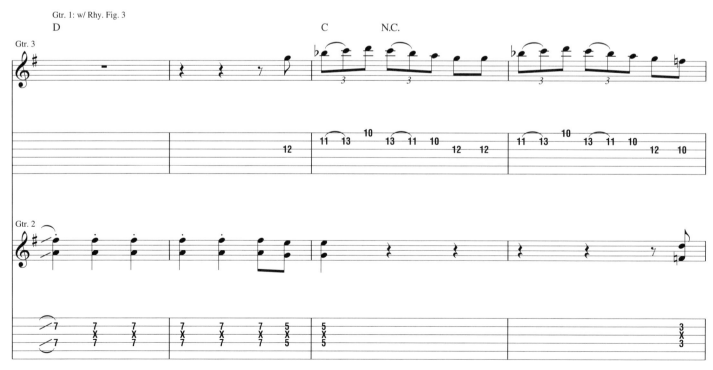

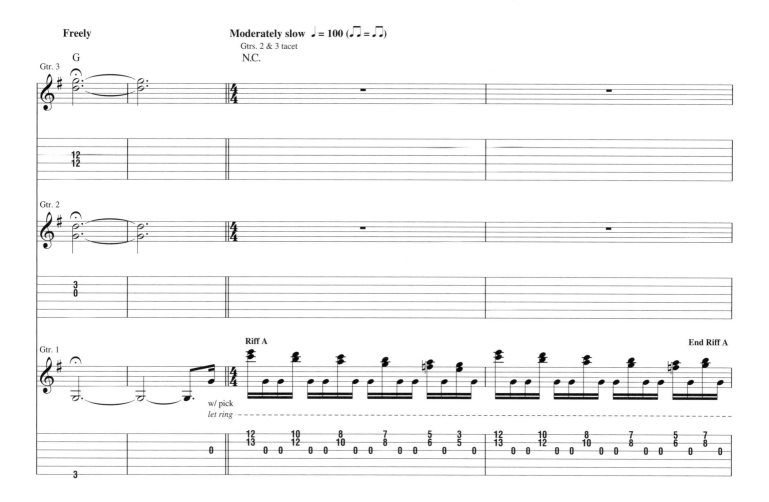

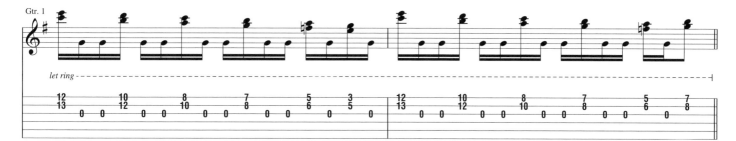

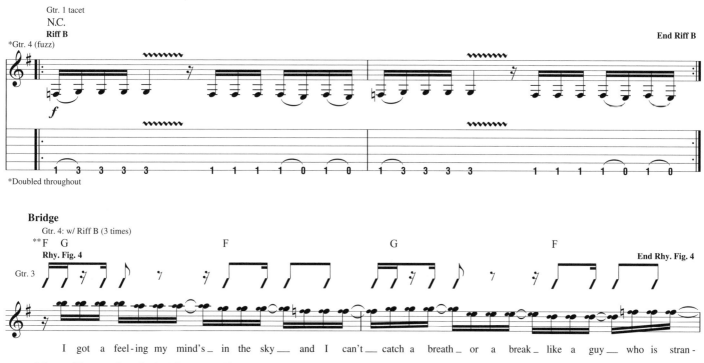

*Doubled throughout

I got a feel-ing my mind's in the sky and I can't catch a breath or a break like a guy who is stran-

**See top of first page of song for chord diagrams pertaining to rhythm slashes.

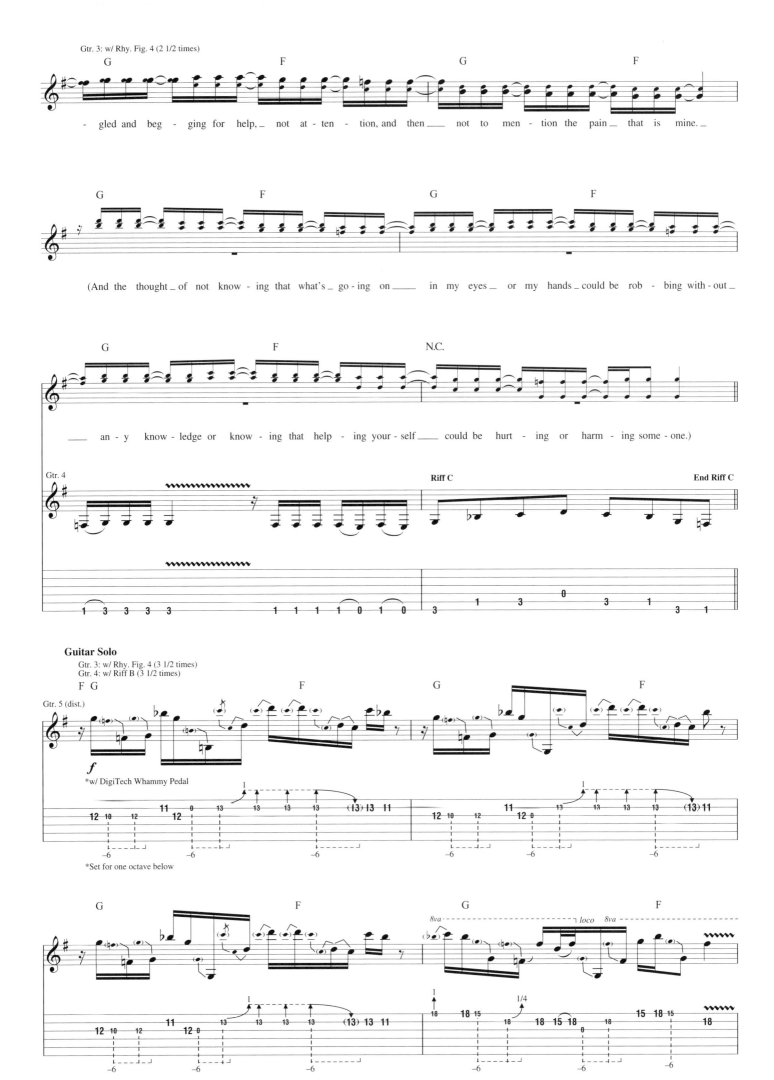

Bridge

Gtr. 3: w/ Rhy. Fig. 4 (4 times)
Gtr. 4: w/ Riff B (4 times)
Gtr. 5 tacet

I got a feel-ing my mind's _ in the sky _ and I can't _ catch a breath _ or a break _ like a guy _ who is stran -

- gled and beg - ging for help, _ not at - ten - tion, and then _ not to men - tion the pain _ that is mine. _

And the thought _ of not know - ing that what's _ go-ing on _ in my eyes _ or my hands _ could be rob - bing with-out _

_ an - y knowl - edge or know - ing that help - ing your - self _ could be hurt - ing or harm - ing some - one.

Interlude

Gtr. 1: w/ Riff A (6 times)

N.C.

Gtr. 4

2

1/3

71

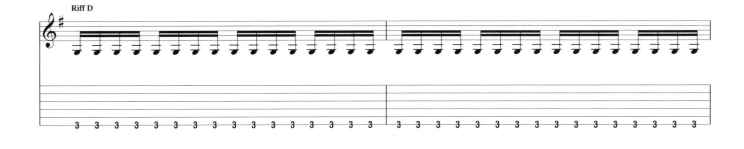

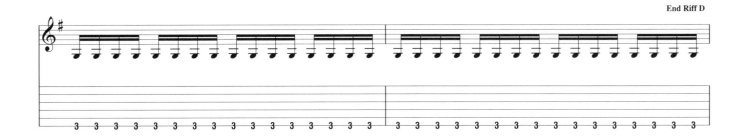

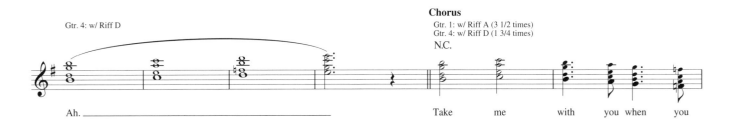

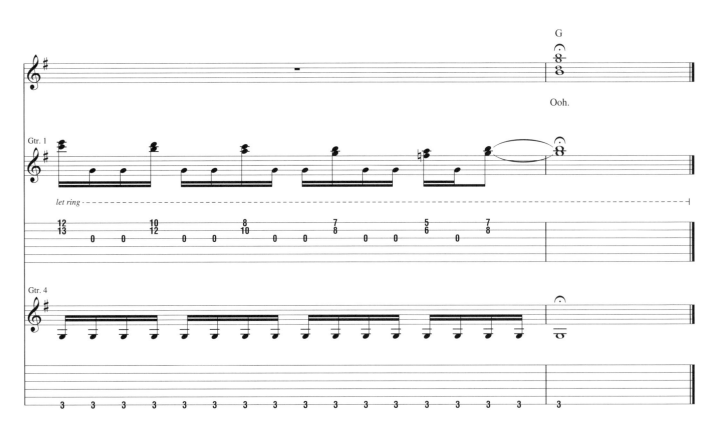